What Are
Rivers?

by Mari C. Schuh

Consulting Editor: Gail Saunders-Smith, Ph.D.
Consultant: Sandra Mather, Ph.D., Professor Emerita,
Department of Geology and Astronomy,
West Chester University,
West Chester, Pennsylvania

Pebble Books

an imprint of Capstone Press
Mankato, Minnesota

Pebble Books are published by Capstone Press
151 Good Counsel Drive, P.O. Box 669, Mankato, Minnesota 56002
http://www.capstone-press.com

1 2 3 4 5 6 07 06 05 04 03 02

Library of Congress Cataloging-in-Publication Data
Schuh, Mari C., 1975–
    What are rivers? / by Mari C. Schuh.
    p. cm.—(Earth features)
    Includes bibliographical references (p. 23) and index.
    Summary: Simple text and photographs provide facts about rivers.
    ISBN 0-7368-1171-0
    1. Rivers—Juvenile literature. [1. Rivers.] I. Title. II. Series.
GB1203.8 .S38 2002
551.48′3—dc21   2001004548

Note to Parents and Teachers

The Earth Features series supports national science standards for units on landforms of the earth. The series also supports geography standards for using maps and other geographic representations. This book describes and illustrates rivers. The photographs support early readers in understanding the text. The repetition of words and phrases helps early readers learn new words. This book also introduces early readers to subject-specific vocabulary words, which are defined in the Words to Know section. Early readers may need assistance to read some words and to use the Table of Contents, Words to Know, Read More, Internet Sites, and Index/Word List sections of the book.

Table of Contents

A river is a body
of flowing water.

The start of a river
is called the source.
A river starts as
a small stream
and becomes wider.

Some rivers bend
and twist.

Rivers move sand
and small rocks.

Some rivers have waterfalls. The water flows from a high place to a low place.

Some rivers have rapids. The water flows quickly over large rocks.

Rivers sometimes flood.
Water flows over
riverbanks and onto land.

Rivers sometimes branch out. Then they flow into lakes and oceans. The place where a river ends is called the mouth.

United States

Mississippi River

The Mississippi River is in the United States. It is the largest river in North America.

Words to Know

flood—to overflow with water beyond the normal limits

flow—to move along smoothly

mouth—the part of a river that empties into a lake or an ocean; the mouth is the end of a river.

rapids—a part of a river where the water flows very quickly; rapids usually have many rocks that the river flows over.

riverbank—the high ground on the sides of a river

source—the place where a river begins

stream—a small body of flowing water; streams join other streams to form a river.

twist—to turn or wind slightly

waterfall—a place where river water falls from a high place to a lower place

Read More

Dwyer, Jacqueline. *Rivers.* Nature Books. New York: Rosen, 2001.

Owen, Andy, and Miranda Ashwell. *Rivers.* Geography Starts. Des Plaines, Ill.: Heinemann Interactive Library, 1998.

Vaughan, Jenny. *Rivers and Streams.* Geography Starts Here. Austin, Texas: Raintree Steck-Vaughn, 1998.

Internet Sites

American Rivers
http://www.americanrivers.org/aboutrivers

Mississippi River States Map/Quiz Printout
http://www.enchantedlearning.com/usa/statesbw/mrstates/ms.shtml

Rivers and Streams
http://mbgnet.mobot.org/fresh/rivers/main.htm

Index/Word List

Word Count: 111
Early-Intervention Level: 14

Credits

Kia Bielke, cover designer; Jennifer Schonborn, production designer and illustrator;
    Kimberly Danger, Mary Englar, and Jo Miller, photo researchers

C. C. Lockwood/Bruce Coleman, Inc., 18, 20
Comstock, 1
© Ecoscene/CORBIS, 16
Frederick D. Atwood, 8
James P. Rowan, 10
Jeff Foott/TOM STACK & ASSOCIATES, 4
John Elk III, 6
Robert McCaw, 14
Sharon Gerig/TOM STACK & ASSOCIATES, 12
Visuals Unlimited/Glenn Oliver, cover